MW01035808

PARAMAHANSA YOGANANDA
(1893–1952)

How to Cultivate Divine Love

by
Paramahansa Yogananda

"How-to-Live" Series
No. 1703

Self-Realization Fellowship
FOUNDED 1920 BY PARAMAHANSA YOGANANDA

A publication of
SELF-REALIZATION FELLOWSHIP
Founded in 1920 by ParamahansaYogananda

ABOUT THE "HOW-TO-LIVE" SERIES: These informal talks and essays were originally published by Self-Realization Fellowship in its quarterly magazine, *Self-Realization*. Some have also appeared in anthologies and on recordings produced by the society. The "How-to-Live" series was created in response to requests from readers for pocket-size booklets presenting Paramahansa Yogananda's teachings on various subjects. The series offers guidance by Sri Yogananda and some of his longtime disciples, Self-Realization Fellowship monks and nuns, many of whom had the opportunity to receive the spiritual direction and training of this beloved world teacher over a period of many years. New titles are added to the series periodically.

Authorized by the International Publications Council of
SELF-REALIZATION FELLOWSHIP
3880 San Rafael Avenue • Los Angeles, CA 90065-3219

Self-Realization Fellowship was founded by Paramahansa Yogananda as the instrument for the worldwide dissemination of his teachings. The Self-Realization Fellowship name and emblem (shown above) appear on all SRF books, recordings, and other publications, assuring the reader that a work originates with the society established by Paramahansa Yogananda and faithfully conveys his teachings.

ISBN-13: 978-0-87612-381-2
ISBN-10: 0-87612-381-7

Printed in the United States of America
1703-J6012

— ✧ —

*There is a Power that will light
your way to health, happiness,
peace, and success, if you will
but turn toward that Light.*

—Paramahansa Yogananda

— ✧ —

How to Cultivate Divine Love

By Paramahansa Yogananda

A talk given at the Self-Realization Fellowship Temple, Hollywood, California, October 10, 1943

The world as a whole has forgotten the real meaning of the word *love*. Love has been so abused and crucified by man that very few people know what true love is. Just as oil is present in every part of the olive, so love permeates every part of creation. But to define love is very difficult, for the same reason that words cannot fully describe the flavor of an orange. You have to taste the fruit to know its flavor. So with love. All of you have tasted love in some form in your hearts; therefore you know a little about what it is. But you have not understood how to develop love, how to purify and expand it into divine love. A spark of this divine love exists in most hearts in the beginning of life, but is usually lost, because man does not know how to cultivate it.

Many people wouldn't think it even necessary to analyze what love is. They recognize love as the feeling they have for their relatives, friends, and others to whom they are strongly attracted. But there is much more to it than that. The only way I can describe real love to you is to tell you its effect. If you could feel even a particle of divine love, so great would be your joy—so overpowering—you could not contain it.

Think deeply about what I am telling you. The satisfaction of love is not in the feeling itself, but in the joy that feeling brings. Love gives joy. We love love because it gives us such intoxicating happiness. So love is not the ultimate; the ultimate is bliss. God is *Sat-Chit-Ananda,* ever-existing, ever-conscious, ever-new Bliss. We, as soul, are individualized *Sat-Chit-Ananda.* "From Joy we have come, in Joy we live and have our being, and in that

sacred Joy we will one day melt again."* All
the divine emotions—love, compassion, cour-
age, self-sacrifice, humility—would be mean-
ingless without joy. Joy means exhilaration,
an expression of the ultimate Bliss.

Man's experience of joy originates in the
brain, in the subtle center of God-conscious-
ness that the yogis call the *sahasrara,* or
thousand-petaled lotus. Yet the actual feeling of joy is experienced not in the head but
in the heart. From the divine seat of God-
consciousness in the brain, joy descends into
the heart center,† and manifests there. That

---

* Taittiriya Upanishad 3-6-1.

† The *anahata chakra,* the subtle dorsal center; the
seat of feeling; center of control of *vayu,* the vibratory
air element, a manifestation of the creative *Aum* vibration. Man's life and consciousness are perpetuated by the
power and activity within the "tree of life," the trunk of
which is seven subtle centers located in the spine and
brain. From these centers comes the power for all man's
physiological and psychological functions and abilities.
Owing to their common center of origin, some spiritual
and psychological experiences are intertwined with physiological processes. For example, there is a definite con-
nection between the physiological function of the heart

joy comes from God's bliss—the essential and ultimate attribute of Spirit.

Though joy may be born in conjunction with certain outer conditions, it is not subject to conditions; it often manifests without any material cause. Sometimes you wake up in the morning "walking on air" with joy, and you don't know why. And when you sit in the silence of deep meditation, joy bubbles up from within, roused by no outer stimulus. The joy of meditation is overwhelming. Those who have not gone into the silence of true meditation do not know what real joy is.

We feel much happiness in the satisfaction of a desire; but in youth we often feel in the heart a sudden happiness that comes as if from nowhere. Joy expresses itself under certain conditions, but it is not created by those conditions. Thus, when someone receives a thousand dollars and exclaims, "Oh,

---

and the subtle spiritual center of feeling in the heart. Working together, they express the great emotion of love, both human and divine.

how happy I am!" the condition of having received a thousand dollars has merely served as a pickax, releasing a fountain of joy from the hidden reservoir of bliss within. So, in human experience, certain events are usually required to bring forth joy, but the joy itself is the perennial native state of the soul. Love also is native to the soul, but love is secondary to joy; there could be no love without joy. Can you think of love without joy? No. Joy attends love. When we speak of the misery of unrequited love, we are talking of an unfulfilled longing. The actual experience of love is always accompanied by joy.

The Universal Nature of Love

In the universal sense, love is the divine power of attraction in creation that harmonizes, unites, binds together. It is opposed by the force of repulsion, which is the outgoing cosmic energy that materializes creation from the cosmic consciousness of God. Repulsion keeps all forms in the manifested state through *maya,* the power of delusion that divides, differentiates, and disharmonizes. The attractive force of love counteracts cosmic repulsion to harmonize all creation and ultimately draw it back to God. Those who live in tune with the attractive force of love achieve harmony with nature and their fellow beings, and are attracted to blissful reunion with God.

In this world, love presupposes duality; it springs from a mutual exchange or suggestion of feeling between two or more forms. Even animals express a certain type of love for one another and for their offspring. In many species, when one mate dies, the other usually succumbs soon after. But this love in animals is instinctive; they are not responsible for their love. Human beings, however, have a great deal of conscious self-determination in their exchange of love with others.

In man, love expresses itself in various ways. We find love between man and wife, parent and child, brother and sister, friend and friend, master and servant, guru* and disciple—as with Jesus and his disciples and the great masters of India and their *chelas*— and between the devotee and God, soul and Spirit.

Love is a universal emotion; its expressions are distinguished by the nature of the thought through which it moves. Hence, when love passes through the heart of the father, fatherly consciousness translates it into fatherly love. When it passes through the heart of the mother, motherly consciousness translates it into motherly love. When it passes through the heart of the lover, the consciousness of the lover gives that universal love still another quality. It is not the physical instrument, but the consciousness through which the love moves that determines the quality of love expressed. Thus a father may express motherly love, a mother may express friendly love, a lover may express divine love.

* See *guru* in glossary.

Every reflection of love comes from the one Cosmic Love, but when expressed as human love in its various forms, there is always some taint in it. The mother doesn't know why she loves the child; the child knows not why he loves the mother. They do not know whence comes this love they feel for one another. It is the manifestation in them of God's love; and when it is pure and unselfish, it reflects His divine love. Thus, by investigating human love, we can learn something of divine love, for in human love we have glimpses of that love of God's will.

Fatherly Love Is Based on Reason

Fatherly love is wisdom-born, and based on reason. Uppermost in the father's consciousness is the thought, "This is my child to take care of and protect." He does this unselfishly, expressing his love by doing things to please and instruct the child as well as providing for its needs. But fatherly love is partly instinctive, as are all forms of familial love; the father cannot help but love the child.

Motherly Love Is Based on Feeling and Is Unconditional

Motherly love is broader. It is based on feeling, rather than on reason. True mother love is unconditional. We can say that in many ways it is more spiritual and therefore greater than most human expressions of love. God implanted in the heart of the mother a love for the child that is unconditional, regardless of the child's merit or behavior. Even if the child in later life becomes a murderer, the mother's love remains steady, unchanged; whereas the father may be more impatient and less inclined to forgive. The unconditional love of the mother is perhaps the human love closest to the perfection of God's love. The true mother forgives her son even when no one else will. That kind of love exemplifies God's love; He forgives His children no matter what sins they have committed. Now who could have placed this love in the mother's heart, save God? In true maternal love God gives us distinct proof that He loves us unconditionally, no matter how wicked we are, or how many times we have sinned.

The Divine Spirit is not a tyrant. He knows He has put us in a world of delusion. He knows we are in trouble; He knows of our struggles. Man only increases the inner darkness of his spiritual ignorance when he thinks of himself as a sinner. It is better for him to try to correct himself, appealing to the Divine Mother for help, beholding in Her the reflection of God's infinite love and forgiveness.

While I was meditating last night, I sang this love song to the Divine:

O Divine Mother, I am Thy little babe, Thy helpless babe, secretly sitting on Thy lap of immortality. I shall steal my way to heaven secreted on Thy lap. In the shelter of Thy lap I shall steal my way to heaven. No karma can touch me, for I am Thy babe, Thy little babe, Thy helpless babe. Secretly on Thy lap I shall steal my way to heaven.

That is the relationship to have with God, for the love of the Mother is the all-forgiving love of the Divine.

Conjugal Love

At its most idealistic, conjugal love can be one of the greatest expressions of human love. Jesus implied this when he said: "For this cause shall a man leave father and mother, and shall cleave to his wife."* When man and woman genuinely and purely love one another, there is complete harmony between them in body, mind, and soul. When their love is expressed in its highest form, it results in a perfect unity. But this love, too, has its flaw; it can be tainted by the abuse of sex, which eclipses divine love. Nature has made the sex impulse very strong so that creation might go on; therefore, sex has its place in the marital relationship between man and woman. But if it becomes the supreme factor in that relationship, love flies out the

* Matthew 19:5.

door and disappears completely; in its place come possessiveness, over-familiarity, and the abuse and loss of friendship and understanding. Though sexual attraction is one of the conditions under which love is born, sex in itself is not love. Sex and love are as far apart as the moon and the sun. It is only when the transmuting quality of true love is uppermost in the relationship that sex becomes a means of expressing love. Those who live too much on the sex plane lose their way and fail to find a satisfying marital relationship. It is by self-control, in which sex is not the ruling emotion, but only incidental to love, that husband and wife can know what real love is. In this modern world, unfortunately, love is too often destroyed by overemphasis on sex experience.

Those who practice a natural—not forced—moderation in their sex life develop other enduring qualities in the husband-wife relationship: friendship, companionship, understanding, mutual love. For example,

Madame Amelita Galli-Curci* and her husband, Homer Samuels, are the greatest lovers I have met in the West. Their love is beautiful because they practice these ideals of which I speak. When parted even for a short time, they eagerly look forward to seeing each other again, to being in each other's company, to sharing their thoughts and love. They live for each other.

The relationship between Ella Wheeler Wilcox† and her husband is another beautiful example of conjugal love. Mr. John Larkin, a student of mine who knew them, told me that he had never seen anything like their love. He said, "Each time they met, it was as if they experienced again the joy of the first time. They were utterly devoted to each other. For three years after his death, her constant

---

* World-renowned soprano (1889–1963) who met Paramahansa Yogananda during his early years in the United States. She and her husband became devoted members of Self-Realization Fellowship. She wrote the foreword to Paramahansaji's book *Whispers from Eternity*.

† American poet (1850–1919).

thought was of reunion with him; then she passed on, his name on her lips."

I met a man of similarly unselfish devotion in this country. He deeply loved his wife, so much so that his love for her became transmuted into divine love. After she died, he wandered for years, seeking a way to find her again. At last he did succeed. In the end, he found God through his love for her. This is the story as he told it to me: In his wanderings after her death, he sought out a great saint in the Himalayas. He persuaded the holy man to promise to give spiritual initiation to him and his wife together. After assuring him of his promise, the saint asked, "Where is your wife?" The husband then told him that she was dead. The saint nevertheless kept his promise to give initiation to the two together. He instructed the man to sit in meditation, and began to invoke the presence of the wife. Suddenly she appeared. For a long time she talked with her husband. Then the two sat together and received initiation from the saint. Afterward, the holy one blessed them, and the wife departed. From that moment, the husband realized that the beloved form he had known as his wife was in reality an individualized manifestation of the consciousness of God—as is every human being. The true meaning of divine love, which is behind and responsible for every ideal human relationship, was revealed to him. His was a unique and true experience.

But conjugal love is tricky, and most people leave this world with an unsatisfied heart. They have not sought marital love in the right way. Attracted mostly by pleasing appearance, they look for their soul mate in a graveyard of beautiful, nicely dressed forms, unmindful that a devil may be housed within. I am not condemning man and woman for responding to the God-created law of attraction; I am condemning the perversion of that attraction through lustfulness. Every man who looks upon a woman as an object of lust, and who abuses woman to satisfy his lust, commits self-destruction: Continued sex-abuse impairs the nervous system and affects the heart, eventually destroying peace and happiness. Mankind must realize that the basic nature of the soul is spiritual. For man and woman to look upon each other only as a means to satisfy lust is to court the destruction of happiness. Slowly, bit by bit, peace of mind will go.

The abuse of sex is comparable to running a car without oil; the body cannot stand it. Each drop of vital essence lost is equivalent to the loss of eight drops of blood. But the important point to remember is to learn self-control. This comes with control and purification of the mind, and is far superior to abstaining outwardly from sex when the mind is yet dwelling on it. Mere suppression can be harmful.

Man and woman should look upon one another as reflections of the Divine. I find it very sweet when a husband calls the wife "Mother," or when she calls him "Father." Every woman should look upon man as a father. My attitude toward woman is as toward a mother. In my eyes she is not merely a woman, but an expression of the Divine Mother. It is Divine Mother I behold speaking to me through woman.

Women should not strive to attract men with "it."* One should always look neat, and it is not wrong to make oneself attractive, if it is done with good taste. But it is wrong to strive purposely to attract the opposite sex through sex appeal. Attraction between man and woman should come from the soul. Those who have sex control and do not flaunt themselves as sex symbols have a much better chance of attracting the right kind of mate. So many young girls have come to me and complained that the boys want sex first or they won't take them out. Sex experience is ruinous to youthful lives. In India, young people never touch or kiss until they are married. Love comes first. That must be the ideal.

* At the time, a well-known catchword for sex appeal.

When two people feel an unconditional attraction for each other, and are ready to sacrifice for one another, they are truly in love. Then only are they ready for an intimate relationship in marriage. Mere possessiveness won't do. When one marriage partner tries to control the other, it shows a lack of real love. But when they express their love in continual thoughtfulness for the true happiness of the other, it becomes divine love. In such a relationship we have a glimpse of the Divine.

Many wives come to me and say, "My husband doesn't want me to become interested in spiritual matters." This is extremely selfish. If the wife is trying to make herself more spiritual, the husband should cooperate with her. He won't lose her; on the contrary, he will receive a part of her virtue. This same principle applies to a woman's attitude toward her husband. The greatest thing a husband or wife can wish for the spouse is spirituality; for soul unfoldment brings out the divine qualities of understanding, patience, thoughtfulness, love.

But each should remember that the desire for spiritual growth cannot be forced on the other. Live love yourself, and your goodness will inspire all your loved ones.

After a few years of marriage, thousands of husbands and wives ask themselves, "Where has our love gone?" It has been burned on the altar of sex abuse, selfishness, and lack of respect. When these qualities enter the relationship, love turns to ashes. Woman nags man when he strives to enslave her, or when she feels he has neglected her. However, tongue lashing is one of the worst treatments one can inflict on another. It is said that a woman's three-inch tongue can kill a man six feet tall. When man and woman mistreat each other, they destroy forever their happiness together. Man should strive to see the God in woman, and to help her realize her spiritual nature. He should make her feel that she is with him not merely to satisfy his sensual appetites, but as a companion whom he respects and regards as an expression of the Divine. And woman should look upon man in the same way.

Another wrong attitude is fear of the opposite sex; abnormal aversion, like abnormal attraction, is an unhealthy attitude. From my master, Swami Sri Yukteswarji,* I learned to regard woman, not as an instrument created for the entrapment and moral destruction of man, but as a representative of the Divine Mother of the Universe. If and when man begins to look upon woman as a mother symbol, he will find in her a loving protection he has never seen before. Through God's grace, I have been able to change the consciousness of many men and women with this spiritual thought: Every man should look upon woman as a symbol of the Mother of the Universe, and every woman should look upon man as a symbol of the Father of the Universe. When those persons left my presence, they felt that the Divine Mother and the Heavenly Father

---

* Paramahansa Yogananda's guru.

had spoken through me, because I addressed them from that divine consciousness.

I wonder if there would be any conjugal love at all, if there were no such thing as sex attraction. Ordinary persons would not have the capacity to feel such love, but those who are spiritually developed would, because they are not attracted on the basis of sex. Those who have cultivated their soul qualities know that sex has nothing to do with true love. If you develop the perfect love of your soul, you will begin to get a glimpse of the Divine. Jesus Christ manifested that love, which is pure and grand and wonderful. This love found expression also in the lives of many great saints.

Love Between Master and Servant

The tie of love between master and servant is based on mutual benefit. The more money and kindness given by the master, the more the servant loves him. The greater the service rendered by the servant, the more warmly the master regards him. This can be a relationship of love, but its basic motivation is the security each gives to the other.

Friendship—Grandest Relationship of Human Loves

The relationship that exists between friends is the grandest of human loves. Friendly love is pure, because it is without compulsion. One freely chooses to love his friends; he is not bound by instinct. The love that manifests in friendship can exist between man and woman, woman and woman, man and man. But in the love of friendship, there is no sexual attraction. One must practice celibacy and absolutely forget sex if one wants to know divine love through friendship; then friendship nurtures the cultivation of divine love. Such pure friendship has existed between saints and between others who truly love God. If you once know divine love, you will never part with it, for there is nothing else like it in the whole universe.

Love gives without expecting anything in return. I never think of anyone in terms of what he can do for me. And I never profess love to someone because he has done something for me. If I didn't actually feel love, I wouldn't pretend to give it; and since I feel it, I give it. I learned that sincerity from my Master. There may be some who do not feel friendly toward me, but I am a friend to all, including my enemies; for in my heart I have no enemies.

Love cannot be had for the asking; it comes only as a gift from the heart of another. Be certain of your feeling before you say to anyone, "I love you." Once you give your love, it must be forever. Not because you want to be near that person, but because you want perfection for that soul. To wish for perfection for the loved one, and to feel pure joy in thinking of that soul, is divine love; and that is the love of true friendship.

The Unconditional Divine Friendship of Guru and Disciple

The relationship between guru and disciple is the greatest expression of love in friendship; it is unconditional divine friendship, based on a shared, singular goal: the desire to love God above all else. The disciple bares his soul to the master, and the master bares his heart to the disciple. There is nothing hidden between them. Even in other noble forms of friendship there is sometimes diplomacy. But the friendship of the guru-disciple relationship is taintless.

I can think of no relationship in this world greater than that which I had with my Master. The guru-disciple relationship is love in its supreme form. I once left his ashram, thinking I could more successfully seek God in the Himalayas. I was mistaken; and I soon knew I had done wrong. Yet when I came back, he treated me as if I had never left. His greeting was so casual; instead of rebuking me, he calmly remarked, "Let us see what we have to eat this morning."

"But Master," I said, "aren't you angry with me for leaving?"

"Why should I be?" he replied. "I do not expect anything from others, so their actions cannot be in opposition to wishes of mine. I would not use you for my own ends; I am happy only in your own true happiness."

When he said that, I fell at his feet and cried, "For the first time there is someone who truly loves me!"

If I had been looking after the business of my earthly father and had run away, Father would have been very angry with me. When I had refused to accept a lucrative position offered to me, he wouldn't speak to me for seven days. He gave me the most sincere fatherly love, but still it was blind. He thought money would make me happy; money would have been the grave of my happiness. Only later, after I had started my school at Ranchi, did

Father relent and say, "I am glad you didn't take that job."

But look at my Master's attitude; even though I ran away from the ashram to seek God, his love for me remained unchanged. He didn't even rebuke me. Yet at other times he always told me clearly when I was wrong. He said, "If my love can be bribed to compromise itself, then it is not love. If I have to alter my behavior toward you for fear of your reaction, then my feeling for you is not true love. I must be able to speak to you honestly. You can walk out anytime, but so long as you are with me I will remind you, for your own highest good, when you are going wrong." I had never imagined anyone could be so interested in me. He loved me for myself. He wanted perfection for me. He wanted me to be supremely happy. That was his happiness. He wanted me to know God; to be with the Divine Mother for whom my heart longed.

Was that not divine love he expressed? to wish constantly to guide me in the path of goodness and love? When that love is developed between the guru and disciple, the disciple has no desire to manipulate the master, nor does the master seek control of the disciple. Supreme reason and judgment govern their relationship; there is no love like this. And I tasted of that love from my Master.

God's Love Sublimely Manifest in Bhagavan Krishna

Lord Krishna expressed in his life pure love in its highest form. He has shown to the world that a love without any impurity can exist between man and woman. It is impossible to describe adequately his life for the general public, because it was unique and transcended mundane laws and standards. Someday I hope to put in print the true significance of Krishna's life, for it has been much misunderstood and misinterpreted. His expression of divine love was unique in this world.

Krishna had many women disciples, but one favorite, Radha. Each disciple said to herself, "Krishna loves me more than anyone else." Still, because Krishna often talked of Radha, the others were envious of her. Noticing their jealousy, he wanted to teach them a lesson. So one day Krishna feigned a terrible headache. The anxious disciples expressed their great concern over the Master's distress. At last Krishna said, "The headache will go away if one of you will stand on my head and massage it with your feet." The horrified devotees exclaimed, "We cannot do this. You are God, the Lord of the Universe. It would be highest sacrilege to dare to desecrate your form by touching your sacred head with our feet!"

The Master was pretending an increase of his pain when Radha came on the scene. She ran to her Lord, saying, "What can I do for you?" Krishna made the same request of her that he had made of the other devotees. Radha immediately stood on his head;

the Master's "pain" disappeared, and he fell asleep. The other disciples angrily dragged Radha away from the sleeping form.

"We will kill you," they threatened.

"But why?"

"You dare to step on the head of the Master?"

"What of it?" Radha protested. "Did it not free him from his pain?"

"For such a sacrilegious act you will go to the lowest stratum of Hades."

"Oh, is that what you are worrying about?" Radha smiled. "I would gladly live there forever if it would make him happy for a second."

Then they all bowed down to Radha. They understood why Krishna favored her; for Radha alone had no thought for herself, but only for her Lord's comfort.

Nevertheless, because she received much special attention, Radha became filled with pride. So one day the Lord Krishna said to her, "Let us steal away together." He played on her vanity, making her think he wanted to be alone with her. She was feeling very happy and favored. They walked some distance, and Krishna wasn't at all inclined to stop for rest. Finally the weary Radha suggested, "Here is a nice place to sit for a while." Krishna looked disinterested and replied, "Let us find a better spot." They walked and walked. At last the exhausted Radha complained, "I cannot walk any further." Krishna said, "All right, do you want me to carry you?" This very much pleased Radha's vanity. But even as she sprang to his back, lo! Krishna was gone; she fell in a heap on the ground. Her pride shattered, on her knees she humbly cried, "My beloved Lord, I was wrong in wanting to possess and control you. Please forgive me." Krishna reappeared and blessed her. Radha had learned a great lesson that day. It was a grievous error to look upon the Master as an ordinary man, to be ensnared and controlled by feminine wiles. She realized that the Master was interested not in her form, but in her soul.

The Perfect Love Between Soul and Spirit

The greatest love you can experience is in communion with God in meditation. The love between the soul and Spirit is the perfect love, the love you are all seeking. When you meditate, love grows. Millions of thrills pass through your heart. If you learn to control sex attraction and attachment to human beings; and if you strive to love all and to meditate more deeply, there will come into your life such love as you never dreamed possible. That is the love that Krishna gave, and that Jesus Christ expressed for all of his disciples. It is the love Jesus had for Mary. Martha worked hard for the Master, but her mind was on the chores, not on him; Mary thought more of the Master himself than of her work. Because of Mary's greater love, Jesus said of her, "Mary hath chosen that good part, which shall not be taken away from her."* And on another occasion, when Mary had brought ointment to anoint the feet of Jesus, and Judas said, "Why was not this ointment sold for three hundred pence, and given to the poor?" Christ answered, "The poor always ye have with you; but me ye have not always."† He accepted Mary's devotion, not for himself personally, but for the Spirit within him. And Mary, by anointing Jesus' feet, was expressing her love for God. That Mary thought first to offer her love to Him who is Master of the Universe, and then to others, shows her good judgment. There is no one to whom we owe love more than to God. And there is no love sweeter than the love He gives to those who seek Him.

So why spend all your time pursuing temporary human love? Conjugal, familial, fraternal—all forms of human love have blind alleys. Divine love is the only perfect love. It is God who is playing hide-and-seek in the

* Luke 10:38–42.
† John 12:2–8.

corridors of hearts, that perchance behind lesser human loves you may find His all-satisfying love.

Therefore love God, not for His gifts, but because He is your own, and because He made you in His image; and you will find Him. If you meditate deeply, a love will come over you such as no human tongue can describe; you will know His divine love, and you will be able to give that pure love to others.

That divine love of God came over me last night. I had only a wink of sleep, so overwhelming it was. In that great flame of love I am beholding you all. Such is the love I feel for you! In your faces I see what is in your hearts.

In the consciousness of one who is immersed in the divine love of God, there is no deception, no narrowness of caste or creed, no boundaries of any kind. When you experience that divine love, you will see no difference between flower and beast, between one human being and another. You will commune with all nature, and you will love equally all mankind. Beholding but one race—the children of God, your brothers and sisters in Him—you will say to yourself: "God is my Father. I am part of His vast family of human beings. I love them, for they are all mine. I love, too, my brother sun and my sister moon, and all creatures my Father has created and in whom His life flows."

True love is divine, and divine love is joy. The more you meditate, seeking God with a burning desire, the more you will feel that love in your heart. Then you will know that love is joy, and joy is God.

PARAMAHANSA YOGANANDA
(1893–1952)

"The ideal of love for God and service to humanity found full expression in the life of Paramahansa Yogananda....Though the major part of his life was spent outside India, still he takes his place among our great saints. His work continues to grow and shine ever more brightly, drawing people everywhere on the path of the pilgrimage of the Spirit."

—from a tribute by the Government of India upon issuing a commemorative stamp in Paramahansa Yogananda's honor

Born in India on January 5, 1893, Paramahansa Yogananda devoted his life to helping people of all races and creeds to realize and express more fully in their lives the true beauty, nobility, and divinity of the human spirit.

After graduating from Calcutta University in 1915, Sri Yogananda took formal vows as a monk of India's venerable monastic Swami Order. Two years later, he began his life's work with the founding of a "how-to-live" school—since grown to seventeen educational institutions throughout India—where traditional academic subjects were offered together with yoga training and instruction in spiritual ideals. In 1920, he was invited to serve as India's delegate to an International Congress of Religious Liberals in Boston. His address to the Congress and subsequent lectures on the East Coast were enthusiastically received, and in 1924 he embarked on a cross-continental speaking tour.

Over the next three decades, Paramahansa Yogananda contributed in far-reaching ways to a greater awareness and appreciation in the West of the spiritual wisdom of the East. In Los Angeles, he established an international headquarters for Self-Realization Fellowship — the nonsectarian religious society he had founded in 1920. Through his writings, extensive lecture tours, and the creation of Self-Realization Fellowship temples and meditation centers, he introduced hundreds of thousands of truth-seekers to the ancient science and philosophy of Yoga and its universally applicable methods of meditation.

Today, the spiritual and humanitarian work begun by Paramahansa Yogananda continues under the direction of Brother Chidananda, president of Self-Realization Fellowship/Yogoda Satsanga Society of India. In addition to publishing his writings, lectures, and informal talks (including a comprehensive series of *Self-Realization Fellowship Lessons* for home study), the society also oversees temples, retreats, and centers around the world; the Self-Realization Fellowship monastic communities; and a Worldwide Prayer Circle.

In an article on Sri Yogananda's life and work, Dr. Quincy Howe, Jr., Professor of Ancient Languages at Scripps College, wrote: "Paramahansa Yogananda

brought to the West not only India's perennial promise of God-realization, but also a practical method by
which spiritual aspirants from all walks of life may
progress rapidly toward that goal. Originally appreci-
ated in the West only on the most lofty and abstract
level, the spiritual legacy of India is now accessible
as practice and experience to all who aspire to know
God, not in the beyond, but in the here and now....
Yogananda has placed within the reach of all the most
exalted methods of contemplation."

HOW-TO-LIVE SERIES
GLOSSARY

ashram. A spiritual hermitage; often a monastery.

astral world. The subtle world of light and energy that lies behind the physical universe. Every being, every object, every vibration on the physical plane has an astral counterpart, for in the astral universe (heaven) is the "blueprint" of the material universe. A discussion of the astral world and the still subtler causal or ideational world of thought may be found in Chapter 43 of Paramahansa Yogananda's *Autobiography of a Yogi*.

Aum (Om). The Sanskrit root word or seed-sound symbolizing that aspect of Godhead which creates and sustains all things; Cosmic Vibration. *Aum* of the Vedas became the sacred word *Hum* of the Tibetans; *Amin* of the Muslims; and *Amen* of the Egyptians, Greeks, Romans, Jews, and Christians. The world's great religions state that all created things originate in the cosmic vibratory energy of *Aum* or Amen, the Word or Holy Ghost. "In the beginning was the Word, and the Word was with God, and the Word was God....All things were made by him [the Word or *Aum*]; and without him was not any thing made that was made" (John 1:1, 3).

avatar. From the Sanskrit word *avatara* ("descent"), signifying the descent of Divinity into flesh. One who attains union with Spirit and then returns to earth to help humanity is called an avatar.

Bhagavad Gita. "Song of the Lord." Part of the ancient Indian *Mahabharata* epic, presented in the form of a dialogue between the avatar *(q.v.)* Lord Krishna and his disciple Arjuna. A profound treatise on the science of Yoga and a timeless prescription for happiness and success in everyday living.

Bhagavan Krishna (Lord Krishna). An avatar *(q.v.)* who lived in India many centuries before the Christian era. His teachings on Yoga *(q.v.)* are presented in the Bhagavad Gita. One of the meanings given for the word *Krishna* in the Hindu scriptures is "Omniscient Spirit." Thus, *Krishna*, like *Christ*, is a title signifying the spiritual magnitude of the avatar—his oneness with God. (See *Christ Consciousness.*)

Christ center. The center of concentration and will at the point between the eyebrows; seat of Christ Consciousness and of the spiritual eye *(q.v.)*.

Christ Consciousness. The projected consciousness of God immanent in all creation. In Christian scripture it is called the "only begotten son," the only pure reflection in creation of God the Father; in Hindu scripture it is called *Kutastha Chaitanya*, the cosmic intelligence of Spirit everywhere present in creation. It is the universal consciousness, oneness with God, manifested by Jesus, Krishna, and other avatars. Great saints and yogis know it as the state of *samadhi (q.v.)* meditation wherein their consciousness has become identified with the intelligence in every particle of creation; they feel the entire universe as their own body.

Cosmic Consciousness. The Absolute; Spirit beyond creation. Also the *samadhi*-meditation state of oneness with God both beyond and within vibratory creation.

guru. Spiritual teacher. The *Guru Gita* (verse 17) aptly describes the guru as "dispeller of darkness" (from *gu*, "darkness" and *ru*, "that which dispels"). Though the word *guru* is often misused to refer simply to any teacher or instructor, a true God-illumined guru is one who, in his attainment of self-mastery, has realized his identity with the omnipresent Spirit. Such a one is uniquely qualified to lead others on their inward spiritual journey.

The nearest English equivalent to *guru* is the word *Master.* As a mark of respect, Paramahansa Yogananda's disciples often use this term in addressing or referring to him.

karma. The effects of past actions, from this or previous lifetimes. The law of karma is that of action and reaction, cause and effect, sowing and reaping. By their thoughts and actions, human beings become the molders of their own destinies. Whatever energies a person has set into motion, wisely or unwisely, must return to that person as their starting point, like a circle inexorably completing itself. An individual's karma follows him or her from incarnation to incarnation until fulfilled or spiritually transcended. (See *reincarnation.*)

Krishna. See *Bhagavan Krishna.*

Kriya Yoga. A sacred spiritual science, originating millenniums ago in India. A form of *Raja* ("royal" or "complete") *Yoga,* it includes certain advanced techniques of meditation that lead to direct, personal experience of God. *Kriya Yoga* is explained in Chapter 26 of *Autobiography of a Yogi,* and is taught to students of the *Self-Realization Fellowship Lessons* who fulfill certain spiritual requirements.

maya. The delusory power inherent in the structure of creation, by which the One appears as many. *Maya* is the principle of relativity, inversion, contrast, duality, oppositional states; the "Satan" (lit., in Hebrew, "the adversary") of the Old Testament prophets. Paramahansa Yogananda wrote: "The Sanskrit word *maya* means 'the measurer'; it is the magical power in creation by which limitations and divisions are apparently present in the Immeasurable and Inseparable....In God's plan and play (*lila*), the sole function of Satan or *maya* is to attempt to divert man from Spirit to matter, from Reality to unreality....*Maya* is the veil of transitoriness in Nature...the veil that each man must lift in order to see behind it the Creator, the changeless Immutable, eternal Reality."

paramahansa. A spiritual title signifying one who has attained the highest state of unbroken communion with God. It may be conferred only by a true guru on a qualified disciple. Swami Sri Yukteswar bestowed the title on Paramahansa Yogananda in 1935.

reincarnation. A discussion of reincarnation may be found in Chapter 43 of Paramahansa Yogananda's *Autobiography of a Yogi.* As explained there, by the law of karma (*q.v.*), the past actions of human beings set into motion the effects that draw them back to this material plane. Through a succession of births and deaths they return to earth repeatedly to undergo here the experiences that are the fruits of those past actions, and to continue a process of spiritual evolution that leads ultimately to realization of the soul's inherent perfection and union with God.

samadhi. Spiritual ecstasy; superconscious experience; ultimately, union with God as the all-pervading supreme Reality.

Satan. See *maya.*

Self. Capitalized to denote the *atman,* or soul, the divine essence of man, as distinguished from the ordinary self, which is the human personality or ego. The Self is individualized Spirit, whose essential nature is ever-existing, ever-conscious, ever-new Bliss.

Self-realization. Realization of one's true identity as the Self, one with the universal consciousness of God. Paramahansa Yogananda wrote: "Self-realization is the knowing—in body, mind, and soul—that we are one with the omnipresence of God; that we do not have to pray that it come to us, that we are not merely near it at all times, but that God's omnipresence is our omnipresence; that we are just as much a part of Him now as we ever will be. All we have to do is improve our knowing."

spiritual eye. The single eye of intuition and spiritual perception at the Christ (*Kutastha*) center (q.v.) between the eyebrows; the entryway into higher states of consciousness. During deep meditation, the single or spiritual eye becomes visible as a bright star surrounded by a sphere of blue light that, in turn, is encircled by a brilliant halo of golden light. This omniscient eye is variously referred to in scriptures as the third eye, the star of the East, the inner eye, the dove descending from heaven, the eye of Shiva, and the eye of intuition. "If therefore thine eye be single, thy whole body shall be full of light" (Matthew 6:22).

Yoga. The word *Yoga* (from the Sanskrit *yuj,* "union") means union of the individual soul with Spirit; also, the methods by which this goal is attained. There are various systems of Yoga. That taught by Paramahansa Yogananda is *Raja Yoga,* the "royal" or "complete" yoga, which centers around practice of scientific methods of meditation. The sage Patanjali, foremost ancient exponent of Yoga, has outlined eight definite steps by which the *Raja Yogi* attains *samadhi,* or union with God. These are (1) *yama,* moral conduct; (2) *niyama,* religious observances; (3) *asana,* right posture to still bodily restlessness; (4) *pranayama,* control of *prana,* subtle life currents; (5) *pratyahara,* interiorization; (6) *dharana,* concentration; (7) *dhyana,* meditation; and (8) *samadhi,* superconscious experience.

BOOKS BY PARAMAHANSA YOGANANDA

Available at bookstores or online at
www.srfbooks.org

Autobiography of a Yogi

Autobiography of a Yogi
(Audiobook, read by Sir Ben Kingsley)

God Talks With Arjuna: The Bhagavad Gita—
A New Translation and Commentary

The Second Coming of Christ: The Resurrection of the
Christ Within You—A Revelatory Commentary on the
Original Teachings of Jesus

The Collected Talks and Essays
Volume I: Man's Eternal Quest
Volume II: The Divine Romance
Volume III: Journey to Self-realization

Wine of the Mystic: The Rubaiyat of Omar Khayyam—
A Spiritual Interpretation

Whispers from Eternity

DVD VIDEO

Awake: The Life of Yogananda
A film by CounterPoint Films

A complete catalog of books and audio/video recordings
—including rare archival recordings of Paramahansa
Yogananda—is available on request or online at
www.srfbooks.org.

FREE INTRODUCTORY PACKET

The scientific techniques of meditation taught by Paramahansa Yogananda, including *Kriya Yoga*—as well as his guidance on all aspects of balanced spiritual living—are taught in the *Self-Realization Fellowship Lessons*. Please visit www.srflessons.org to request a comprehensive complimentary information packet about the *Lessons,* which includes:

- *"An Overview of the Self-Realization Fellowship Lessons: Information About Paramahansa Yogananda's Home-Study Series"*

- *"Highest Achievements Through Self-Realization,"* by *Paramahansa Yogananda—a thorough introduction to the teachings presented in the SRF Lessons*

SELF-REALIZATION FELLOWSHIP
3880 San Rafael Avenue • Los Angeles, CA 90065-3219
TEL (323) 225-2471 • FAX (323) 225-5088
www.yogananda.org

Also published by Self-Realization Fellowship...

AUTOBIOGRAPHY OF A YOGI
by Paramahansa Yogananda

This acclaimed autobiography presents a fascinating portrait of one of the great spiritual figures of our time. With engaging candor, eloquence, and wit, Paramahansa Yogananda narrates the inspiring chronicle of his life—the experiences of his remarkable childhood, encounters with many saints and sages during his youthful search throughout India for an illumined teacher, ten years of training in the hermitage of a revered yoga master, and the thirty years that he lived and taught in America. Also recorded here are his meetings with Mahatma Gandhi, Rabindranath Tagore, Luther Burbank, the Catholic stigmatist Therese Neumann, and other celebrated spiritual personalities of East and West.

Autobiography of a Yogi is at once a beautifully written account of an exceptional life and a profound introduction to the ancient science of Yoga and its time-honored tradition of meditation. The author clearly explains the subtle but definite laws behind both the ordinary events of everyday life and the extraordinary events commonly termed miracles. His absorbing life story thus becomes the background for a penetrating and unforgettable look at the ultimate mysteries of human existence.

Considered a modern spiritual classic, the book has been translated into more than fifty languages and is widely used as a text and reference work in colleges and universities. A perennial bestseller since it was first published more than seventy years ago, *Autobiography of a Yogi* has found its way into the hearts of millions of readers around the world.

An award-winning documentary film about Paramahansa Yogananda's life and work, *Awake: the Life of Yogananda*, was released in October 2014.

"A rare account." —THE NEW YORK TIMES

"A fascinating and clearly annotated study."
—NEWSWEEK

"There has been nothing before, written in English or in any other European language, like this presentation of Yoga."
—COLUMBIA UNIVERSITY PRESS